WALT DISNEY PRODUCTIONS

Disney Colour Library

HOW IT HAPPENS

PURNELL

A Fishy Dish

We all know that fish comes from the sea. But do you know how it gets to your dinner table? Well, fishermen go to sea in fishing boats. The largest of these are called "trawlers." Every captain has a brave crew.

Fishermen sometimes stay at sea for as long as six weeks. When storms blow up, the fishermen's work goes on, even if they are sea-sick (poor Donald!). Huge nets are thrown over the side of the ship to catch the fish.

When the nets are full, they are hauled up and emptied into the ship's hold. Everyone should stand clear. The fishing boat then returns to harbour.

The fish is unloaded and sent to the shops. Fishermen are proud to see their fish being sold.

The fish is taken home and eaten. Do you like fish? Donald, Daisy, Huey, Dewey and Louie all do!

Your Daily Bread

Everyone loves big slices of bread and butter. But who makes it for you? The baker, of course. A lot of our bread is made in large bakeries, and each baker does a small part of the breadmaking. First the dough-makers mix the dough, taking care not to fall in (as Brer Bear has).

When the dough is mixed, men called table-hands knead it.

The dough is put into baking tins, and the oven man puts them into a furnace oven. Because of the great heat, he uses a long pole to put the loaves in.

When the loaves are baked, they are taken to bread shops. Maybe you live near a small baker who sells his bread while it is still warm.

How To Look After Your Pet Dog

It is important to look after your dog properly. You must always feed him well, even if you go short yourself.

Nights can be very cold, so your dog should have a warm kennel. "A plate of soup and a hot-water bottle will keep any dog happy and comfortable," chuckles Pluto.

Make sure your dog has plenty of exercise. He will soon say "Time for walkies!"

Always keep your dog on a leash. He will love long walks, and sometimes a good, fast run.

Take good care of your dog and he will be your best friend — always lovable and loyal.

The Elephant's Trunk

The mighty elephant is very clever in the various ways he uses his long trunk. For instance, he can uproot big trees.

He can pluck a little flower without damaging a single petal.

He can lift his master and place him safely on his back.

He can pick the tastiest leaves from the top of a tree when he is hungry.

When he is thirsty, he sucks water into his trunk, then squirts it into his mouth.

And he takes a bath by squirting water all over himself. Next time you visit the zoo, watch how the elephant uses his trunk.

How a House is Built

It is important that a house should be built on firm, dry land. Marshy land just won't do.

After a man called an architect has drawn up plans of the house a bulldozer levels the ground.

When the founda-
tions are laid, the
walls are built with
a space between the
bricks to keep the
house warm and
dry.

The big tim-
bers which will
support the
roof are ham-
mered into
position.

Finally, the
painters paint
the woodwork,
electricians in-
stall wiring,
and the car-
penters put in
windows and
doors.

How The Cowboy Got His Horse

Five hundred years ago there were no horses in North America. The Red Indians were bored because they had to stay in camp and help with the chores.

One day, gallant knights on horseback arrived. At first the Indians thought the horse and its rider were one animal!

Then one day a horse threw its rider off, and the Indians decided to fight the white men and take their horses.

During the fighting some horses escaped. They ran off and lived wild. Then white ranchers decided to capture the wild herds and sell them. Cowboys were hired to round up and tame the horses. This was hard, because the horses did all they could to throw their riders. They were called "broncos", which is a Spanish word meaning rough and bad-tempered. And so the cowboy got his horse!

How Bananas Reach The Fruit Shop

Bananas grow in hot countries, such as the West Indies. The bunches are cut down while they are still green but they are not good to eat yet!

Then they are loaded on to special cargo ships, where they are kept in a cold room to ripen slowly on the way to Britain.

In this country the bananas are put on to a railway train and taken to a sorting depot. (The Big Bad Wolf has caught a bunch that has fallen off the train.)

Then they are sorted into bunches called "hands" and packed into boxes to be delivered to the green-grocer. They are now properly ripe and ready to eat.

Milk—From The Cow to Your Doorstep

Milk comes from cows, so the cows must be milked. This can be dangerous, as cows sometimes like to kick. Most farmers avoid this by using a milking machine.

The milk is poured into churns and taken to a dairy, where it is tested and made germ-free. Then it is bottled and taken to the depot.

At the depot *your* milkman loads his van with crates of bottles, then sets out on his round.

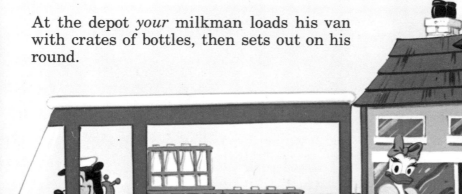

The milkman comes every day, so you can be sure that your milk is always fresh and good to drink.

Taking Honey From a Bee-hive

To collect honey the bee-keeper protects his face from bee-stings with a fine veil. He takes with him a "smoker".

He lifts the roof off the hive and quietens the bees with puffs of smoke. If this doesn't work, he will leave in a hurry and wait for the bees to settle down again.

Bees make their honey-combs on frames which the bee-keeper has placed inside the hive. He removes these frames and the honeycombs.

The honey is extracted and poured through muslin filters to clean it. This leaves small bits of wax and dirt behind. After a few days the honey can be eaten.

Saved From The Sea

Sailing can be fun, but if a sudden storm blows up it can mean trouble. Coastguards are always on the lookout for anyone in danger. This one has just seen a sailing boat about to sink.

The coastguard telephones the Royal Air Force helicopter service, and the crew rush to take off at once.

The crewmen are pilot, navigator and winchman. After sighting the wreck the winchman is lowered by the navigator on the end of a winch.

Reaching the sinking yacht, he fastens a harness called a "strop" around one of the people to be rescued. They are both hauled up to the helicopter. This action is repeated until everyone has been saved.

Mounting a Horse

Mounting a horse is not easy. It is an old custom to mount from the left. Knights used to wear their swords on their left hip, and if they mounted from the right their swords could get tangled between their legs.

Sometimes film-stars leap into the saddle. Never try this. The animal might move, and you would miss completely.

When you mount, hold the reins in your left hand. If you don't the horse might turn his head and bite your leg.

Always put your left foot in the stirrup. If you use your right foot you will land back to front. It isn't easy, is it?

Making a Dog Basket

For thousands of years baskets have been made from rushes grown in marshy ground.

The rushes are sorted into different lengths and thicknesses. They must be kept well soaked at this point, otherwise they will split.

Then the baskets are woven. Here a dog basket is being made.

Dogs are very fond of their baskets. *"Don't they look sweet, tucked up so neat, in a dog basket made for two?"*

Other titles in the series

ABC

Nursery Rhymes

People You See